DEDICATION

I dedicate this work to these friends who have been a model of God's grace and character in my life:

Diane Moder
Jane Hansen Hoyt
Diane Fink
Susan Boucard
Clara Wilkins

God has used each of you in shaping my character and my life.

Thank you for all you have been to me personally and thank you for reflecting His image so beautifully throughout the Body of Christ.

Thank you Sherry Gilmore, my special friend and publishing buddy who always believed this would happen. Your support has been priceless.

Love to each of you, Jennie

CONTENTS

When my kids were little and got sick, like any good Mom I would get out the medicine that I knew would make them feel better and get well. I can still see that little face as I approached, remedy in hand. In a flash, my child's mouth clamped shut, and his lips pressed together so tight that a breath could barely pass through them, much less the teaspoon of medicine I was holding!

As grown-ups, we often don't like to take the "medicine" of God's Word for the things that ail us as human beings. However, in her book, At The Core, Jennie Newbrough offers us a remedy to help us to understand those areas in our character that can hinder us from being all God intends for us. If ever there was a bottom line, "rubber-meets-the-road" concern for us as believers, it must be the issue of character. "Defects of character" are the things that ail us and Jennie lovingly uncovers them for us. We must let our character confront us, Jennie says. Not always easy. Yet with warmth and tenderness, Jennie leads us from the places of brokenness that have wrongly shaped our character, to a vantage point of hope where we can see a future filled with promise.

Sharing her personal experiences and weaknesses in a way that is honest and self-disclosing, she reveals the openness and vulnerability that is the hallmark of her own transformed character. She is a woman we can all relate to! Jennie has been a Christian counselor for 25 years, a part of the Aglow ministry for even longer, but more importantly, she has been a friend and a great encourager in my life for many years.

I know that as you read this book, your life will be touched, and your character transformed…AT THE CORE!

Jane Hansen Hoyt
President/CEO
Aglow International

A SPECIAL NOTE TO THOSE DOING THE COURAGEOUS WORK OF RECOVERY

12 Step programs such as Celebrate Recovery, wisely include the step in which we *"give God permission to remove our defects of character."* However many people do not recognize exactly what "defects of character" are, so they do not fully benefit from this vital step of their recovery. One of the purposes of this book is to help those doing the brave work of recovery with this crucial step.

I respect you and hope this book will help you fulfill your journey of recovery.

The Road to Recovery was not meant to be traveled alone.

I am honored to walk along side you.

Why...

"The shape of your character is the shape of your future."

—Erwin Raphael McManus

The seriousness and significance of this statement are why this material is being written.

Character is "at the core" of who we are. And at the root of all problems are the "defects of our character."

In our modern culture, character is an obscure dynamic, not truly understood nor highly valued. Many things in our current culture are considered "relative" to an individual's particular beliefs or choices. Character is also often viewed as something relative when in reality it is the most significant part of each of our lives.

Character is at the very heart, center, or core of who we are as individuals. Character is what the Bible says God looks upon in each of us (1Samuel 16). Your character determines your destiny.

I want a life shaped by integrity and godliness and filled with purpose and wholeness. I want a Christ-shaped character that gives glory to God.

I invite you to join me in this destiny shaping quest for character.

Jennie Newbrough

CHAPTER ONE

The Maker

A few years ago I read a little story that left a big impression. As I thought of how to begin writing on character, I remembered this story of the trees, and decided to let the trees introduce you to this work on character.

A Story of Two Trees

Two trees stood on a hill. One stood tall and straight. Its velvet leaves shimmering in the wind, revealing alternating soft and slick surfaces. Its trunk gleamed, and the birds nested within its full set of branches.

The second tree was shorter. Its branches and leaves were compact and sparse compared to those of the beautiful tree. Few birds nested among its leaves, but several bird families had made their homes in various holes in the trunk. The short tree's roots entwined themselves among the rocks and clawed at soil wherever it could be found.

"What's wrong with your trunk?" asked the beautiful tree.

"You mean this hollow section?" said the old tree. "This was from the fire of 1906. I went up in flames and thought I was a goner. Fortunately, the rains came and quenched the fire, leaving me at the edge of this meadow with a lovely view and many new friends like yourself."

"Thank you for the compliment," said the beautiful tree. "And why are you leaning to the side?"

"My lean allows me to see my roots more clearly," said the old tree. "It happened in 1936. A tornado came through here, ripping and tearing. I tell you, I was scared. All the beautiful young trees were tossed about and mangled. It was a tragic day. I almost met my Maker myself. If it hadn't been for that drought in 1925 that made me extend my roots deep and wide, I'd have been killed for sure. It's kind of you to ask about me."

"I've always prided myself on my compassion," said the beautiful tree. "Excuse me, but I couldn't help but notice: You don't seem to spread much pollen around. You're not sick, are you? I'm not going to catch any disease from you, am I?"

The old tree laughed and shook its leaves hard. "No, I'm just getting old. I have been blessed with seeing many of my saplings raised. But sadly, many have fallen. I've found that there are some things that I simply can't control in life. It has been difficult for me to adjust to. Thank you for being concerned about my health."

"It's nothing, really. Would you like for me to tell you about my history? It's fascinating.

"I would indeed," said the old tree and listened patiently for the next hour.

In the afternoon, a storm blew in from the west. The beautiful tree stood defiantly and righteously, awaiting its chance to pit its strength against the winds. The old tree hunched its leaves together and thought of the painful events of the past and of the benevolence of its Maker.

When the wind swept through with terrible destructiveness, the beautiful tree was stripped of its velvet leaves, and its trunk cracked. "Why?" it asked the old tree.

"The Maker doesn't explain why," said the old tree. "The Maker just builds character."

~~~~~~~~~~~~~~~~~

I love this story of life told through the trees. How often we, too, ask, "Why?" Why has God allowed certain difficult things to happen? Why have we gone through the specific storms of life that we have?

Graham Cooke says, "To the heights God wants to take you… will be the depths He will also take you in terms of character development." Francis Frangipane writes, "Adversity does not perfect character, it reveals character. It expresses what is happening inside of us."

Dr. Ronald Cottle says in his wonderful book, *Anointed to Reign*, "God will never lead you to do anything that is contrary to His character. In God's Kingdom, both ends and means must be in line with divine character." He continues to say, "Anytime you take your destiny into your own hands, you are taking God's will past God's character. Anytime you take God's will or work past His character, you will have problems."

Our Maker is forming character. His character, the character of Christ, is being formed in us.

Jane Hansen Hoyt, leader of Aglow International, says this so well in her book. *Fashioned for Intimacy*. She writes, "Because God is a Father, has the nature of a Father and is alone the source of all goodness. He wanted to reproduce Himself and fill the earth with His own image-all that He is. All of His characteristics-His love, His gentleness, His mercy, His grace-were attributes of a Father for

His children, attributes that He intended to reproduce in them. He wanted all creation, especially 'the principalities and powers in heavenly places,' to be able to look at His family and His children and recognize that God was indeed their Father. In them, the beauty of His Father-heart and nature would be displayeds (see Eph.3:9-11). This gives greater meaning to the words we read in Genesis 1:26 when God said, 'Let Us make man in Our image, according to Our likeness.'"

Jane concludes, "The heart, or spirit, of each human being is where God desired to dwell, where He would reveal Himself to bring growth and change in our lives. God reproduces His likeness in the heart."

In our story, the Old Tree said that the Maker doesn't say why, He just builds character. But our "why" is answered in Hebrews 12: 3-11. God loves us as His children and He disciplines us "that we may be partakers of His holiness," and "it yields the peaceable fruit of righteousness to those who have been trained by it" (NKJV).

Holiness and righteousness are the great "whys" of our story. This is the character of Christ.

The good news is that the Maker will continue His work in you. In Philippians 1:6, the apostle Paul says it this way "being confident of this, that he who began a good work in you will carry it on to completion until the day of Christ Jesus."

As you read the following material, may you understand the work of the Maker within you; may you be encouraged to endure as His character is formed in you.

May we, as the Old Tree, each become humble and wise and endure to help others.

THINK ABOUT IT

1. Which are you more like right now in your life, the young tree or the old tree?

2. Are you asking "why" or are you learning to trust? What are your "whys"? List the areas you know you are trusting.

3. How conscious are you that you have "character"?

4. Now that you are thinking about character, who in your life has character that you admire? What is it that you admire?

CHAPTER TWO

Life Happens

I had been invited to be a speaker at a retreat in the state of Idaho. I had never been to Idaho and did not realize what a journey it would be. There were no direct flights from Pittsburgh, Pennsylvania to Idaho, so I believe I changed planes around three times and finally arrived by a small propeller plane at a remote airport on the desolate prairie somewhere in Idaho. I was fine and just happy to be on the ground.

My experience, however, was not quite over. The solitary attendant at the airport met me with a big apology. The ladies who were to pick me up had arrived a bit earlier and she had mistakenly told them my plane would be delayed another two hours, so they had left and would return in two hours. I understood and was content to buy a Coke and walk around the tiny airport and wait. At least I was on the ground.

Two hours passed and my welcome party arrived. As they loaded me and my luggage into the car, they were all apologetic. I assured them it was not a problem and that I was just glad to be with them.

We then began the 2 hour ride to the retreat location. As we traveled my companions began to debate the ordeal. The front seat was sure that the confusion was the result of the enemy (Satan) creating problems and the back seat believed that the whole situation was somehow God at work. To my amusement, they debated this for quite awhile and then someone turned and asked me, "Well, Jennie, what do you think?"

I had listened long enough that I had formed an opinion, but it was different from either of theirs. Not sure they would like my thoughts, I risked it anyway. I began, "I don't think it is either Satan or God. I believe that life sometimes just happens." There was silence in both the front and back seat as they awaited my explanation. "I believe that we bring God or the enemy into it with our response. For me the question is, Who will I be when life happens? Will I respond from my Christ nature or out of my human nature which may agree with the enemy? It really is my choice."

My response gave them a lot to continue to talk about until we arrived at our destination. Upon arriving, they asked me if I would share this very issue at the retreat. I did and we all grew and learned through it.

The question, "Who will I be when life happens?" is the foundational question for our study on character. Life happens and we react, respond and engage in someway.

Once I was laughingly sharing with Clara, a very special and wise friend of mine, about how I had reacted with anger and bitterness in a situation. I concluded my story by saying, "I can't believe I said those things. That just isn't me?"

With the wisdom she is so noted for, she lovingly spoke truth to me, "It can't come out of you if it's not in you." Oh, the power of truth!

When our buttons are pushed, what will be the response? As my wise friend stated, if it is in us, it will eventually come out. When it does, the Lord wants us to face it and deal with it. We can rejoice if our response is righteous or repent if it is not. But we must face who we are. We must let our character confront us. God lovingly lets life happen so we can see ourselves.

I had another airport experience recently. I was flying to Seattle and while waiting in the Cincinnati, Ohio, airport for a connecting flight I saw a bookstore and decided to browse the display of new books. The title of one caught my eye. It was, *I Hope They Serve Beer in Hell.* I was amused by the title, wondering what the book could be about. As I picked up the book I saw that it was championed by the *New York Times*; that means it is selling a lot of copies and the author is making some money. I turned the book over to read the back cover.

This is what the author had to say about his book: "My name is Tucker Max and I am an a—hole. I get excessively drunk at inappropriate times, disregard social norms, indulge every whim, ignore the consequences of my actions, mock idiots and posers, sleep with more women than is safe or reasonable, and genuinely act like a raging d—head. But I contribute to humanity in one very important way: I share my adventures with the world."

All of his words were spelled out; he left nothing to the imagination. He was explicit and I was offended.

Here, promoted by the *New York Times* is a blatant example of poor character paraded as exciting and acceptable. The *New York Times* said on the front that the book is highly entertaining and thoroughly reprehensible. The advertiser and the author admit to the negative nature of the behavior they exploit, yet they exploit it anyway.

Another new book was sent to me by a good friend a few weeks ago. It is not promoted by the *New York Times* and was given away free at a conference. Its title also amused and captivated me. The title is *Deadly Viper*. Its subtitle is "Character Assassins." It is a Christian book and on the back of it the authors introduce it as "a kung fu survival guide for our integrity. proceed with caution." The authors, who are a pastor and his friend, use a martial arts concept to call each of us to spiritual warfare concerning our character. I love their basic concept which is that we must be accountable to a group of safe significant others as protection for our character. By choosing accountability we surround ourselves with strength that guards and confronts our character choices.

In a section of their book called, "No Lone Rangers," they say,

"It is also important to understand this book isn't just about you and your deal. Character is both a personal AND a community concept. If you are a person of great character all those around you benefit. The organization, the relationships, the families: they all win. If you lack character, everyone pays. The building of character is a community thing. There are no Lone Rangers. We need to train together, fight together, and watch each other's backs. True leaders make tough decisions to battle for integrity together no matter how inconvenient or how it may stretch us." (*Deadly Viper*, page 18)

These two transparent warriors go on to say, "Most of us are simply not inclined to talk about our struggles, our inadequacies, and our vulnerabilities with each other. This is counter culture. But we must. We must defend each other in this battle and carry each other's burdens." (*Deadly Viper*, pages 18-19)

Life Happens. And when it does we are vulnerable. We need one another. In the recovery program I am part of, we say, "the Road to Recovery was not meant to be traveled alone." We encourage accountability and group support.

God has also written a book and in it He has some things to say about how we need one another. In the New Testament alone, the term "one another" is used over fifty-one times. We are to be there, one for another. There is safety is numbers. We are called to be an army. We are to stand together. In Ecclesiastes 4:9-12, the Lord says,

"Two are better than one,

because they have a good return

for their work:

If one falls down,

his friend can help him up.

But pity the man who falls

and has no one to help him up!

Also, if two lie down together, they

will keep warm.

But how can one keep warm

alone?

Though one may be overpowered,

two can defend themselves.

A cord of three strands is not

quickly broken."

When life happens I hope you are not alone.

When life happens I hope you will let someone be there for you.

Because... life happens.

THINK ABOUT IT

1. Think about the last time "life happened": How did you react?
2. What did it reveal about your character?
3. Do you agree or disagree with my thoughts about when life happens?
4. Who in your life are you accountable to?
5. Who do you stand with and support in their character development?

CHAPTER THREE

Marked

You have heard comments like these:

> "You can always count on her."
>
> "He is a man of great integrity."
>
> "She is always so nice."

And you have also heard these:

> "He is just plain lazy."
>
> "She is a liar."
>
> "He really has a temper."

These common comments that you make about others and that others may make about you are what it means to be "marked." When a pattern is developed in a person's life, it marks them and we all think of them that way. We become known by the marks we bear., just like the old tree in our story was known by its marks.

The term marked originated from the times when a craftsman would leave his mark on the object he was creating. He formed the mark with a stylus or tool that left a print or groove in the object and it was then marked as his craftsmanship. The mark was called the character of the craftsman. Every piece he created proudly bore his mark. Furniture companies today still mark their pieces with their names. A very common mark is a person's signature. Artists sign their name to mark each piece of their art. You can probably think of other marks that are commonly seen. Business logos and slogans are contemporary marks we all are familiar with.

The Marks

As individuals we are each marked by the most dominant and influential people or situations in our lives. We are also marked by our temperament type and personality and by the personal choices we make. We will be looking at all of these markings.

Probably the first mark left on you was the mark of words spoken by your parents. I was just with my daughter and granddaughter and was pleased to hear my daughter marking her little girl with words of affirmation and confidence.

As my granddaughter would do something as simple as putting a top on a bottle, my daughter would say, "Good job!" She repeated those words of praise each time the little one did the same thing. As a mother she was affirming her daughter's efforts and my granddaughter would repeat the effort over and over to the sounds of her mother's encouragement.

I complimented my daughter on her patience and praise and she said to me, "I learned from the best."

It was true; I had been an affirming parent when my children were growing up. Even when they would do wrong, I would say, "You are better than that." I was pleased to see that a legacy of affirmation had been formed and that we were marking one another with encouragement.

However, all of this has another side. Once when my son was in an angry place as a teen he turned to me and said, "You are just too damned nice!" This was a great learning experience for me. He did not respect me for being nice when he needed me to be strong. This marked me as weak in his eyes. I realize now that I was afraid of his anger and being "nice" was my codependent way of trying to control his anger. My codependency marked me as weak.

In some families negative and abusive words are what we hear as a child. These definitely mark us in significant ways. We then vow "we will never" do what was done to us. But because the mark is there in our soul, we find ourselves doing the very thing we hate.

Can you identify?

We each have patterns, cycles, habits, routines, manners, a bent, a persuasion, a predisposition to do things a certain way. We each have repeated ways we respond to the issues of life. You may do yours consciously or unconsciously. What matters is that you have them and they define and form your character in some way. From my family stories you can see that I have a pattern of being affirming which is a good character trait. But when I am afraid, my affirming ways give way to the weakness of codependent people-pleasing.

We each have character traits. Some are good and some are not. Your patterns, ways, manner of doing things define your character to others.

I think of a group of people I know. I can count on Susan to have things ready. I know Paul will show up late and David will be on time. I expect Mary to be complaining about something and Kathy will have a smile for everyone. Ellen will be withdrawn and her husband, Tom, will be talking too much. If you were in my group what would characterize you?

How to undo these negative patterns and be the person we want to be and were created by God to be is our challenge.

We can only change ourselves. No matter how much I want Paul to be on time, Ellen to be happy, or Mary to quit complaining; I cannot change them. I cannot change the character traits of others; but I can choose to yield to God and work with Him to change the parts of my character that mark me in unhealthy, unproductive, ungodly ways. It is my choice what marks I continue to let corrupt my character. It is your choice how you continue to be marked.

I had a great eighth grade teacher who actually caused us to enjoy memorizing poetry. One of those verses I still remember is by Robert Burns, a 1700 Scottish poet, who wrote,

"O would some power the gift to give us to see

ourselves as others see us."

We do not have the gift to see ourselves as others see us. So we must rely on others to help us see ourselves. People are probably always commenting to you on things about yourself. The issue is "are you listening?" I recommend that you humbly ask a few honest friends. I would also recommend that you pray and ask God to show you how He sees you. He is your very best friend. You can count on Him to speak truth in love.

Not Manufacture Defects

The negative, unhealthy or counter productive marks we have are called "character defects." Every person has both strengths and weaknesses in their character make-up and as we recognize the defects we understand what God is working to change in us. Character defects are what make our life difficult. They arc what set us up to sin, to fail, to struggle. Our character defects are not beneficial; they undermine our life. But most of us do not know how to recognize the defects of our character. They are so much a part of our life that we just think of them as "this is who I am."

But you do not have to remain that way.

God is our Creator and He has not made us defective. It is important to realize that our character defects are not manufacture defects.

Defects began marking God's creation in the Garden of Eden when Eve listened to the voice of the deceiver, the liar. Jesus tells us in John 8:44 that Satan is "a liar and the father of lies."

Satan lied to Eve and she listened. What voices we listen to, what words we take in and receive in our hearts, have power over us.

The Word of God says that out of the mouth come both blessing and cursing (James 3:10). It also says in James 3:6, "The tongue also is a fire, a world of evil among the parts of the body. It corrupts the whole person, sets the whole course of life on fire, and is itself set on fire by hell."

The father of lies, through the words of significant people, marks our soul and shapes how we think of ourselves, our choices of behavior, and the character that becomes who we are.

Yet, there is a greater, more significant mark that makes all the difference.

Christ MARKS you

The good news is that God, your Creation Father, has not created you defective. The marks of the enemy and the marks from other people are not the most significant marks upon your life. The most

31

significant marks were left at creation by your heavenly Father. Only the Creator truly knows the creation. Only God truly knows you and He marks you with:

Forgiveness
Love
Mercy
Acceptance
Adoption
Healing
Deliverance
Grace
Peace
Meekness
Joy
Etc.

God created you in His image and will restore you to His original design (Ephesians 5:27), "Without stain or wrinkle or any other blemish, but holy and blameless."

THINK ABOUT IT

1. What are you revealing about yourself?

   Are you known as loyal, faithful, trustworthy, patient, gentle, humble, caring, giving, confident, peaceful, open, disciplined, sensitive, friendly? Circle those that mark you.

   From this list, circle the ones that mark you: angry, impatient, fearful, irresponsible, selfish, narcissistic, judgmental, neglectful, procrastinating.

2. What MARKS you? What do you believe has most marked your life?

3. Are there specific words that have marked your life? Write them down. Do you think you still believe them, follow them, react to them?

4. How do you see that God has marked your life? List the specific ways that come to your mind.

CHAPTER FOUR

Adding to This

There is more that we must add to our understanding of ourselves. Personality and character must be defined and distinguished from one another. This will give greater understanding of character formation and character defects. Personality and character are related but distinct from one another, yet they do have overlapping dimensions in our lives.

Personality: the enduring pattern, cycle, or style by which one thinks, feels, and relates to others and to one's self. Example – you are either an introvert or an extrovert.

Character: moral qualities – honesty, patience, courage, perseverance, loyalty, and so forth that reflect your trustworthiness in relation to others. Example – you are either dependable or irresponsible.

To Clarify: We express the content of our character through our personality.

Therefore, what you express to others through your personality is what marks you. You reveal your character through your morality, standards, and nature. You become "known" as this type of person. We call it your reputation.

One More Thing:

Besides your personal life experiences and personality there is your Temperament Type which is very significant in your character formation.

Temperament Type – is the basic human nature of a person, the peculiar emotional and mental bent of an individual. As with character, your temperament is seen through your personality, but is distinct from it.

There are four basic temperament types: Sanguine, Choleric, Melancholy, and Phlegmatic. Each type has specific characteristics that individuals with that temperament type display in their life. Each person also has a secondary temperament and will have some characteristics of that type as well.

Since we are examining "character defects," I will list the common defects or weaknesses found in the distinct temperament types. It is important to note that not every person will have all of the specific characteristics of their type, but they will have the majority of the characteristics from their type.

For example, my primary temperament type is Sanguine and two common negative characteristics that I do not have are being messy and being emotionally unstable. But two that I do have are being impulsive and undisciplined. From my secondary temperament type, Choleric, I can be bossy and self-sufficient.

What I am establishing is that the weaknesses of each temperament type are the basis for what we call "character defects."

As you look at the following list, see if you recognize yourself.

Temperament Type Weaknesses:

Sanguine –	Choleric –
Undisciplined	Self-sufficient
Impatient	Cruel/critical
Impulsive	Hot-tempered
Messy	Bossy
Compromising	Task-oriented
Inconsistent	Egotistical
Emotionally unstable	Unsympathetic

Phlegmatic -	Melancholy –
Procrastinates	Over analytical
Passively stubborn	Unforgiving
Self-righteous	Negative
Fearful	Manipulative
Avoidant	Self-centered
Uncommunicative	Introspective
Indecisive	Moody

(There are more weaknesses with each type, but this list gives you a good picture of the issue.)

The good news is that according to Paul:

"You were taught, with regard to your former way of life, to put off your old self, which is being corrupted by its deceitful desires; to be made new in the attitude of your minds; and to put on the new self, created to be like God in true righteousness and holiness."   — Ephesians 4:22-24

We are not bound by the defects of our human nature. We have a new nature in Christ and we can choose to live from this new nature. This is all summed up best in Colossians 1:27, "Christ in you, the hope of glory."

Our new nature (in Christ) is described in Galatians 5:22-23-the fruits of the Spirit of Christ:

Love	Patience	Gentleness
Joy	Kindness	Faithfulness
Peace	Goodness	Self-control

God reveals that He overcomes the weaknesses of our human nature by giving us a new nature in Christ. It then becomes our choice and challenge to exchange our old nature which is so natural to us, so familiar, and oh, so comfortable for this new nature that is so right, yet so different from what and who we are used to being.

I was just talking with a young woman who was being challenged to change her pattern of anger and defensiveness and she said with such agony and despair, "But this is who I am; I don't know how to be any different!" You can probably identify with those thoughts.

I picture myself in a dressing room. The Lord is just outside the dressing room door ready to hand me the new garments of His wonderful nature, but first I must take off the old, that which has been comfortable and seems to fit who I think I am.

I realize that taking off the old is easier said than done. I am glad that God is there to help in the process. He has the strength to tug off that tightfitting garment of the past and the gentleness to adjust me to the new fashion of His ways.

Even as I write this, the seasons are changing and I am putting away the garments of the season past. This is exactly what God is doing. He brings you to a new season of life and says the garments of the past season are not right for you.

With His help I have hope for a change of character and the new life it will bring.

THINK ABOUT IT

(Two good resources for additional understanding of temperment are: The Spirit Filled Temperament, by Tim LaHaye and The Temperament God Gave You, by Art and Laraine Bennett)

1. What most seems to mark you at this time in your life? Your past, your temperament, or your Christ nature? **Write down what you recognize.**

2. What temperament type do you believe you have?

3. Can you identify two or three character defects that you want changed? Be honest. It will help you begin to change. Write them down so you can better recognize them when they show up in your behavior.

4. In prayer, give God permission to remove the "defects." Then be ready to yield when He encourages you to change your thoughts and behaviors.

CHAPTER FIVE

Changing Shape

Recently I had the privilege of hearing a message by Erwin Mc-Manus, pastor of Mosaic Church in California. In his very engaging message he made this most arresting statement:

"The shape of your character is the shape of your future."

This challenging concept brings us face to face with the significance of character. Our future hinges on our character. This truth applies to individuals, to families, to organizations, to ministries, and even to nations. Character defines destiny.

When character is moral, noble, and honorable, the future has hope. But when character is weak, defective, and negative, the future is marked with difficulty.

A hinge is usually small and unnoticed, yet it is powerful. The hinge controls access and movement. The word hinge means held to, controlled by, maneuvered by, attached to, and moved with. Defects of character formed in your past will control, maneuver, and manipulate your future. Our future swings in the direction of the hurts, habits, and hang-ups of our past. Character has the power to direct the future. Character is the hinge.

The good news is that hinges can be replaced.

In Philippians 3:10-16 (AMP), we are encouraged to know that "We are resurrected with Christ..." God is resurrecting us from our past with all of its choices and wounds into our future in Him. Christ raises us from death unto life. Our resurrection is from deadly character to a new nature in Christ.

To choose new life we must first recognize—realize—what the old life has been. This is called coming out of denial. It is necessary, yet not easy. I will show you this process in layers.

On the surface and most easily recognized is our:

Behavior—Self-destructive/self-defeating
Isolation, controlling anger, lying, stealing, addictions, compulsions, avoidance, etc.

Behavior—Constructive/life-giving
Honesty, patience, faithfulness, kindness, generosity, etc.

Underneath our behaviors are:

Character Defects
Low self-esteem, arrogance, fearfulness, selfishness, self-protection, etc.

Character Strengths
Integrity, dependability, openness, selflessness, humility, etc.

At the bottom of it are all our:

Wounds, Issues of Life, and Temperament
(From childhood, significant relationships, trauma, spiritual influence, etc.)

The layers are meshed together and may be hard to separate, but I will try to untangle them with an example. I will use the issue of anger because we all experience it.

Anger is an emotion, generated by our thinking (either conscious or subconscious), resulting in a behavior. Angry behavior may be displayed passively but still be destructive such as obsessive shopping, overeating, drinking, etc. Or anger may be displayed with aggressive outbursts of words and actions. Both are displays of anger; both are destructive. One hurts inwardly, the other, outwardly. The saying is true, "hurt people hurt people."

The passive display of anger may be generated by low self-esteem coming from childhood rejection or it may be selfishness coming from a phlegmatic temperament. The aggressive anger may come from arrogance generated by a choleric temperament or may be fearfulness coming from childhood abuse.

Not all character defects have wounds beneath them. Some individuals have patterns of thinking that have no base in an actual wound or experience. The person simply has formed a false belief. They may believe they are ugly and avoid close relationships because they tell themselves they will be rejected; yet no one has ever rejected them because of their appearance. Sadly, the wound is self-afflicted by faulty thinking.

These are examples of the issues. There could be multiple examples because we all have diverse dynamics that form different combinations; but ultimately we each express anger through our combination of issues.

The Cycle

We must honestly face our character. Our character will have strengths and weaknesses. The strengths we want to build on and enhance, such as honesty, dependability, generosity, faithfulness, kindness, etc. But the weaknesses must be faced and overcome or they will undermine our future.

I have developed what I call The Cycle of the Ultimate Lie. In this cycle we see that Satan, the enemy of our soul, has looked for an access point to imbed a lie. The access point is a wound or issue of life or a temperament weakness. It is an opening to our soul.

The lies are always familiar thoughts:

"I will never be loved."

"I'm not good enough."

"I don't matter."

"No one cares."

"I'm not wanted."

"I'm bad."

"I am a failure."

"I should never have been born." Etc.

You have heard them.

From these marks – access points – come the lie and from the lie comes a cycle of feelings, thoughts, and then behaviors that cause us to agree with the lie. Character defects take shape from the lie and our lives take on a cycle of self-defeat.

God desires that we would be willing to hear and believe His truth about who we are. His truth will set us free from the cycle and from the wounds of our past. The truth frees us from the past to live a new life with a renewed character that leads us into a new future of promise and purpose.

Wounds are real, lies are strong, but truth is ALL-POWERFUL!

In Ephesians 6:10-11 and 14, we are instructed that truth is part of our armor for the battle of life, "Finally, be strong in the Lord and in his mighty power. Put on the full armor of God so that you can take your stand against the devil's schemes….Stand firm then, with the belt of truth buckled around your waist."

God is showing us that truth supports us, enables us to stand, and gives us strength. This is all essential if we are to overcome our familiar defects of character and be a new person possessing our future with a new shape of character.

Changing shape means I must: Hear the truth

See the truth

Believe the truth

Live the truth.

Truth sets me free when I "know" it. To know means that I become intimate with it. I take it in and let it conceive new life in me. Our truth is found in God's Word.

Christ, the divine Carpenter, redeems by replacing my destructive hinges with the new hinge of godly truth.

THINK ABOUT IT

Following is the Cycle of the Ultimate Lie mentioned in this chapter. This cycle will show you the picture we have been describing. Take time to think through the cycle with your own life in mind.

1. What do you recognize as your Ultimate Lie?

2. What truth will set you free?

THE CYCLE OF THE ULTIMATE LIE

Wound or Mark
Opens you to the lie

Shame
Leads to agreement with lie

Feelings & Fears
Thoughts & beliefs produce

Sinful Behaviors
Produce shame

**Your
Character Defects**

Truth
Sets You FREE

Wound or Mark
Opens you to the lie

Break Cycle
Agree with Truth

Feelings & Fears
Thoughts & beliefs produce

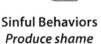

Sinful Behaviors
Produce shame

**Your
Character Defects**

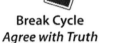

CHAPTER SIX

In the Beginning

Mankind was originally created in God's image. This means that our character defects are not manufacture defects. God did not create us defective. So where and when did these defects enter the picture?

The Garden of Eden was a great place with great people, but in this great garden was also a great deceiver.

Adam had been given a command to "Rule over…every living creature that moves on the ground" (Genesis 1:28).

This command to Adam included dominion over the deceiver. The deceiver, in the form of a serpent, spoke to Eve and she listened. She listened to a voice that spoke contrary to the voices of God and Adam. This voice spoke doubt and deception to her. And she listened.

Eve listened to the voice and it seduced her human nature. As she listened, she heard that God was withholding something from her: "'You will not surely die,' the serpent said to the woman. 'For God knows that when you eat of it your eyes will be opened and you will be like God, knowing good and evil'" (Genesis 3:4-5).

According to the deceiver, she could have more than what God offered. She could be like God. Eve bit into the fruit of deception. The first "defect of character" was exposed and it was PRIDE.

This brought the shame of nakedness and Eve hid herself from God. This avoidance and SELF-PROTECTION was her second "defect." Then God questioned her hiding and she blamed the serpent. The third defect was revealed; it was BLAME-SHIFTING.

How quickly character unraveled once the process began.

Adam failed to take dominion over the deceiver. His sin of disobedience exposed his first defect, IRRESPONSIBILITY. Then Adam also SELF-PROTECTED and he also BLAMED. The downward spiral of defects had been set in motion.

What this familiar story reveals for us is that when we put other voices before the voice of God, we run the risk of being deceived. Deception reaches into our soul and draws upon our human nature. We then respond from our human character rather than the character of Christ within us. We are coping with life on our own rather than by the Spirit of God.

I often wonder what might have been different if Adam and Eve had not given into the defect of SELF-PROTECTION. Had they instead come face-to-face with God and confessed their sins and admitted their defeat by the deceiver, would the consequences of the fall have been different?

We will never know those answers, but I do know what God wants from us today. When or if we listen to the voice of the deceiver, the Word of God encourages us in Hebrews 4:15-16, "For we do not have a high priest who is unable to sympathize with our weaknesses, but we have one who has been tempted in every way, just as we are—yet was without sin. Let us then approach the throne of grace with confidence, so that we may receive mercy and find grace to help us in our time of need."

God does not want us to be controlled by our defects and rely on our humanness. He is calling us to come boldly to Him and receive mercy and grace. Like Adam and Eve, we will sin, but we do not need to hide, to self-protect.

Adam failed to take dominion over the deceiver, but Christ did not. Christ overcame the voice of the deceiver in the wilderness (Matthew 4:1-11). He has been through that encounter and He understands our weaknesses because He came in the likeness of man.

Reliance on Christ is not weakness.

Reliance on Christ is wisdom.

Christ is "the way, the truth, and the life" (John 14:6 NKJV).

THINK ABOUT IT

1. Who do you more identify with: Adam? or Eve? In what ways? List the ways you identify and the effects it has in your life. Be honest with yourself.

2. Think of a time when the deceiver spoke to you. What did your response reveal about your character? If defects of character were revealed, take it to God right now and let Him cleanse you with forgiveness and let Him strengthen you.

CHAPTER SEVEN

Voices

Many voices compete for our attention. The voice we listen to is the one whose servant we become.

We have looked at the issue of voices in Eve's life and we have talked about truth. I now want to bring them together through God's challenge to us in Joshua 24.

A dramatic choice is presented by Joshua to the people of God and this same challenge and choice is ours each and every day. At this time, Joshua knew he was soon to die and that he had to prepare the people, so He gave them three choices: "choose for yourselves this day whom you will serve, whether the gods which your fathers served that were on the other side of the River, or the gods of the Amorites, in whose land you dwell. But as for me and my house, we will serve the Lord" (Joshua 24:15 NKJV).

Joshua discerned for them the voices of three fathers. He challenged them to choose a father's voice to follow. You have the same choice in your life today.

One voice was the voice from their father's land. The voice heard in "our father's land" is what we heard spoken to us in our childhood home. It has left a strong impression on our mind and self-image. If that voice was affirming and full of loving discipline and guidance, we are blessed. Too often the voice from "our father's land" is full of rejection or indifference that continues to echo into our adulthood.

The second voice is of the god of the world in which you live. According to the Bible, the father of lies is the prince of this world. The father of lies, who is also the accuser, will speak words of failure and rejection, pride and temptation. His voice will also agree with all negatives we heard in "our father's land."

The third voice is the voice of our Creation Father, the Lord God Almighty. What the Creator says about His creation is the truth, for He has fashioned it and formed it. The Creator is the one who truly knows the creation. This is the only voice of truth. This is the voice of your truth.

We choose. We choose each day, many times a day, which voice we will follow, which voice will be the god of our life. But if we do not recognize the difference in the voices and the source of the voice we can be misled and greatly deceived.

The Israelites had learned well under Joshua's leadership. They learned to trust the voice that Joshua served. Their response to Joshua's challenge was, "'The Lord our God we will serve and His voice we will obey!'" (Joshua 24:24 NKJV).

A healthy self-concept and identity grow from knowing I am loved and accepted, that I have value, and that my life has meaning and purpose. God's voice reveals these truths to us. They are God's heart for each of us. Let us believe His truth and obey His voice.

Listen to His Word speaking your truth.

Genesis 1:26 – "Then God said, 'Let us make man in our image…'" You are God's idea. He has formed you to be like Him, just like your Creation Father.

2 Corinthians 5:17 (NKJV) – "Therefore, if anyone is in Christ, he is a new creation; old things have passed away; behold, all things have become new." You get a brand new start through Christ; the past is over and gone and all things about you are new.

Ephesians 1:6 (NKJV) – "To the praise of the glory of His grace, by which He made us accepted in the Beloved." You are loved and accepted through Christ.

2 Corinthians 5:21 (NKJV) – "For He made Him who knew no sin to be sin for us, that we might become the righteousness of God in Him." You are righteous through Christ.

John 1:12-13 (NKJV) – "But as many as received Him, to them He gave the right to become children of God…" You are God's own child.

Jeremiah 29:11 (NKJV) – "'For I know the plans I have for you,' declares the Lord, 'plans to prosper you and not to harm you, plans to give you hope and a future.'" You have a destiny with God.

Then in the book of Revelation, the ultimate purpose of God is revealed. He has chosen you as the Bride for His Son: Revelation 19:7-8 – "Let us rejoice and be glad and give him glory! For the wedding of the Lamb has come, and his bride has made herself ready. Fine linen, bright and clean, was given her to wear."

You are chosen.

The Bridegroom, Christ Jesus, will not be unequally yoked. The Father is about the good work of changing your character so He can present you to His Son, as a spotless Bride.

To be like Christ is to have the character of Christ. Our entire purpose in letting God remove our defects of character is that we may then have the character of His Son.

We are being restored to what God intended in the beginning. We were created to be like Him, in His image.

The Apostle Paul, who had many defects of character before he became new in Christ, tells us that we can be confident in this truth, "that he who began a good work in you will carry it on to completion until the day of Christ Jesus" (Philippians 1:6).

God's voice over us is the wonderful voice of love and promise and truth.

THINK ABOUT IT

1. What voice did you hear in your "father's land"? How has it affected you?

2. Other than God's voice, what voice are you aware of serving?

3. Of the words of God's truth listed above, which is hardest to believe? Why?

4. How can believing God's voice change your character?

CHAPTER EIGHT

The Syndrome

I do not remember when, but awhile ago I realized that Satan, the enemy of our lives, is not creative. He has no new strategies, weapons, or ideas. Only God Almighty is creative. And the Almighty wants us to be wise concerning the enemy.

In His Word, God reveals to us the strategies of the enemy, his tactics, his weapons, his ways. When we are discerning, we recognize them. We must be aware that there is a spiritual battle. We are not to be focused nor absorbed with the enemy, but wise and discerning.

The Esau Syndrome is one of the enemy's tactics. So very long ago, when Jacob and Esau were young men, God exposed this work of the enemy in Genesis 25. Here Esau gives up his birthright for a single meal. Think of it! He gave up his entire inheritance, his future blessings, his destiny, for one single serving of stew.

Esau was controlled by his appetite.

What do you have an appetite for? What grabs you? What says NOW? You have to have it now! What desires control you? What can't wait? What occupies your mind? What demands to be fed?

A strong warning is given to us in Hebrews 12:16 in the Message Bible, "Watch out for the Esau syndrome: trading away God's life-long gift in order to satisfy a short-term appetite. You well know how

Esau later regretted that impulsive act and wanted God's blessing – but by then it was too late, tears or no tears."

Here the Esau syndrome is defined – "**trading away God's life-long gift in order to satisfy a short-term appetite.**" How easy it is for us to lose perspective, to think only in the here and now and forget the big picture of life. We think of today, the immediate, and lose sight of the eternal.

We also devalue the long-term. The waiting somehow causes us to forget the true value of what is yet to come. We think of what is right in front of us and it seems so much more significant and essential than what is being stored up for us.

In Genesis 27, Esau wants his father's blessing but it is too late. The blessing, his future, has been given to Jacob. Blessing and birthright go together. In the culture in which Esau lived, he understood this. He knew that his birthright represented all he was entitled to as the firstborn son; the largest part of the family inheritance was to be his. He knew that before his father died the birthright would be given to him through his father's words of blessing. His father would speak the words that represented his future. His father would prophecy his future and it would indeed come to pass.

Birthright and blessing: we, too, have a birthright as children of God and a blessing that comes from God the Father through Christ Jesus, the Son. Our future is foretold to us through Christ. We have the security of eternal life with Him. We have the inheritance of His name, His authority, His protection, His Spirit, His wisdom, His guidance, His unfailing love, His steadfast provision, and His abiding presence.

Like Esau, we will be tempted through our appetites to compromise, to place immediate pleasure before eternal promise.

Let us be quick to learn from our brother Esau.

Let us not fall victim to the syndrome.

Godly character is not controlled by appetite. Godly character is patient, long-suffering, gentle, kind, and self-controlled.

Godly character can see beyond the immediate to the eternal.

THINK ABOUT IT

1. What are your short-term appetites? List them. Be honest with yourself.

2. What have you "traded away" in the past because of these appetites?

3. What do you believe is your inheritance in Christ? Write down what you know God has for you. Pray and ask God to deliver you from the Esau syndrome.

CHAPTER NINE

Sorting It Out

We have looked at the complex dynamics of character and behavior and see that they are connected but distinct at the same time. We will now look at an example to show how it works together.

Our example is with procrastination. (I am sure you don't procrastinate but you might know someone who does.) You know you are responsible to take care of something, pick up the package or pay the bill, but you deliberately put it off and your delayed action frustrates others or costs them in some way.

Here is both a sin and a character defect working together. Like Adam, you are not fulfilling your designated responsibility. The deliberate failure to fulfill a responsibility or promise is sinful. But if this is a pattern in your life and it happens frequently and others begin to say, "I can't count on you" or "You are so frustrating," then you have developed a "character defect."

Sin is usually the symptom of the **defect of character**; it is what we see. But when there is a repeated pattern of the sinful behavior, a character defect has formed.

This is why it is important to correct and discipline children so that their behaviors do not become patterns and then "defects of character." This is why God says in Hebrews 12:10-11, "but God disciplines us for our good, that we may share in his holiness. No discipline seems pleasant at the time, but painful. Later on, however, it produces a harvest of righteousness and peace for those who have been trained by it."

Some sins detailed in God's Word are lust, anger, murder, bitterness, adultery, lying, slothfulness, strife, ambition, envy, drunkenness, idolatry, jealousy, etc. (Galatians 5:19-21).

Some character defects also detailed in God's Word are fear, lying, pride, insecurity, self-protection, irresponsibility, deception, conceit, etc. (Found in multiple places and stories of God's people.)

You can see that there is a clear correlation between the lists and that often the behavior is also a "defect." Lying is on both lists. When we tell a lie, which we have all done, we sin. But when we develop a pattern of lying and become deceptive, it then is a "character defect." We become marked as a liar, someone who is not truthful and cannot be trusted.

John Baker, who founded the Celebrate Recovery program at Saddleback Church in California, admits to having been an alcoholic. His alcoholism was the sin, but he identifies low self-esteem as the primary "defect of character" that led him to drink. He drank to coverup his low self-esteem. As he became an alcoholic and his life fell apart, the shame and guilt actually perpetuated his low self-esteem rather than overcoming it.

I have a friend who isolates herself as a form of self-protection. She fears rejection, so she isolates. Her self-protection is a character defect and the fearfulness that motivates the self-protection is another defect of her character. Sometimes fear is just an emotion that appropriately fits a situation; but, in her case, fearfulness is a pattern of thinking and living and is a defect.

One of my character defects is insecurity. I fail to be who God says I am because of my fear of man. I am a people pleaser. Fearing man, putting man before God, is a form of idolatry. Insecurity is the defect that motivates me to commit the sin of idolatry.

Oh! Truth hurts! But facing the truth will set me free.

What does God want us to do with all of this? He wants us to honestly face our defects and confess our sins and give Him permission to remove our defects of character.

As I have mentioned, people will often try to change by not committing the sin anymore. An alcoholic will decide to get sober and not drink any longer. Sobriety is necessary and good. But sobriety is not full recovery. Any recovery program tells you that when the character defects are still within the person and life gets stressful (life happens), as it always does, the defect sets you up to relapse or to choose some other form of sin to cope with life. A friend of mine has been sober from alcohol for five years, yet he still withdraws and avoids responsibility, and that causes as much conflict in his marriage as his drinking did. He has not fully recovered because he has not dealt with the defects of his character.

God wants to transform our character so we are truly changed, fully free from the inside out.

God wants to get to the very root of the problem. We sometimes are content to just coverup the problem, but He goes to the core of it all. We might settle to sweep it under the rug, but God pulls up the rug and removes the dirt altogether.

A beautiful young professional woman I know has a family history of addiction. She became addicted to cocaine, a powerful drug of choice, as a teen. Even while addicted she finished college and seemed to be doing well, but one day her parents found her near death from a cocaine overdose. They placed her in a recovery program and for sixty days she was abstinent from drugs and alcohol, but on the very night she celebrated sixty days of sobriety, she relapsed and went back to cocaine and alcohol.

The good news was that she did not like herself as an addict this time. She became willing to do more recovery and let God remove her "defects of character." She now has completed one full year of recovery, has a good relationship with God, and her future is looking good.

God also recently arranged for me to have an unexpected encounter with a remarkable woman of God whom He used to challenge me to finish this book; her name is Mary Forsythe. Mary gave me a copy of her book, *A Glimpse of Grace*. Her captivating personal story is a graphic picture of how God will use whatever it takes to remove the defects of our character.

Listen to this amazing statement that Mary makes, "I would be leaving prison as an entirely different woman than I had been when I arrived, thoroughly changed from the inside out. What wonders I had seen – and what a miracle I was! I had to go to prison to be set free" (*A Glimpse of Grace*, page 244.)

As I read Mary's book and was challenged to be honest with God and myself, I saw this verse from James 1:12 working itself out in her life, "Blessed is the man who perseveres under trial, because when he has stood the test, he will receive the crown of life that God has promised to those who love him."

One of the most inspiring things you can do for yourself is to get a copy of Mary's book and see through her story of character transformation what God is doing in your character and your story.

THINK ABOUT IT

1. Sin or defect? List two that you see in yourself. Be honest.

2. Have you been working with God to change? In what ways?

3. What defect stands out in your life? When did the pattern begin? How has it damaged your life and relationships?

4. As you read Mary's story, what do you most identify with?

CHAPTER TEN

Coping

When the people and issues of life "mark" us, we respond; we react in a definite way. We may be very aware of our reaction, or it may be very subtle and we are not even conscious of our response. But we do respond.

Over time we develop a pattern of response. For me, I have recognized that a common "mark" is disapproval. As a child, my mother would address me with a tone of disapproval, and now as an adult, I am still very sensitive to disapproval from people.

In a recent situation, God opened my eyes to see myself in a situation of disapproval. A very important person in my life whom I worked with at my church spoke some strong words of disapproval to me and my immediate impulse was "to shrivel up and disappear." God revealed to me that when I hear words or an attitude of disapproval my instinctive response is to "shrivel up". I feel very small and unloved and unimportant and I want to "disappear," to go away, quit, stop being involved or present, withdraw from the person or situation, self-protect in any way possible.

My emotional impulse in this situation was to withdraw from involvement in the group and then to leave the group altogether. My unhealthy thinking is that if I just go away then the people who disapprove will get what they want and I will be safe because they can't hurt me any longer.

As a child, when my mother dispensed her disapproval, I would withdraw for hours and have my personal pity party. And it seemed to work. No one came looking for me. It seemed to be the right thing to do. It seemed to be what everyone wanted. It supported my ultimate lie that I wasn't wanted.

This whole dynamic is what is called coping. We develop patterns of responding and reacting that are termed coping mechanisms. We may call them our idiosyncrasies, personality quirks, or attitudes. But really they are our coping mechanisms that become patterns of behavior and "defects in our character."

These coping patterns are very powerful in our lives. I realize that the personal pattern I have described has caused me to be a "quitter" all my life. I feel unwanted, doubt myself, and quit. Not realizing her words fed the problem, my mother would often say, "Aren't you ever going to finish what you start?"

Webster defines coping as "dealing with or contending with." So we each develop patterns of contending and dealing with the issues of our life. And, as in my example, these patterns may not be healthy. When they are not healthy and we continue them, we create dysfunction and defeat in our lives.

I have a very good friend who for years would, in loving aggravation, confront me, "Why do you do that?" I would not recognize what I was doing and she would repeatedly draw my attention to the fact that if a strong, influential person, especially a woman, came into the situation I would pull back and become very silent. I realized that inside I just wanted to be very small and not be noticed. To be noticed would be to risk disapproval from this powerful person.

This was such an automatic response in me. I would do it without even thinking about it. As my friend drew it to my attention, I could see my behavior, but I didn't stop it. My coping mechanism was very strong.

Coping mechanisms can seem wise. I mean, why would I want to set myself up for disapproval?

The problem was that I was being controlled by fear. And worse than that, I was failing to be who God had called me to be. The fear of man controlled me. I was not living out of God's love for me. I was not living out of His truth for me as we described in chapter seven.

What I am exposing to you is a list of my "character defects." In this situation they are fear of man, self-protection, and low self-esteem. Not a pretty picture!

But I am pleased to share with you that because of my work in recovery and the willingness to overcome my defects of character, God has shown me His way to break this pattern.

I began to pray over the situation at church that I mentioned earlier in this chapter. As I prayed, asking God what to do, He kept giving me a question to ask Him. I would talk to God about the situation, go over and over it and then hear myself say, "How do I grow through this?"

God wanted me to grow. He did not want me using my former "coping mechanisms." I did not want to be the same either. I wanted to overcome. As I pursued the question, "How do I grow?" God began to lead me through this process:

1. He confirmed that I had genuinely received disapproval. He actually said I had been "insulted." This validation of the pain was helpful.

2. He caused me to see my "shrivel-up-and-disappear" pattern as weak and wrong, and I wanted to change.

3. He challenged me to "grow" by going to the person who insulted me and telling them, in a lovingly firm way, that they had hurt me but that I forgave them and that I would NOT receive their insult.

4. He strengthened me to stay in my place of ministry, not "shrivel up" and not "disappear" but actually rise up and be who I knew God was asking me to be with the confidence and courage of Christ.

I have seen God bring great growth in me and in my areas of responsibility as I have obeyed Him.

This has been a tremendous victory for me. It feels so right to handle things like an adult woman of God rather than a wounded child. I am free from the stronghold of longstanding character defects. I am very aware that the fear of man does not control me in the same ways any longer.

I now realize that the concept of coping is deceptive. I wasn't coping. I was in bondage. I was in bondage to the "marks" of my childhood and to the defect of character that developed from them. I was a slave to fear and weakness.

God is good! I had to face the defects to get free, but His freedom is wonderful.

When I went to face the person who "insulted me," I told them I had come to thank them. And I sincerely meant that. I am thankful that God let it all happen so that He could use it to challenge my character.

The Apostle Paul explains it this way, "When I was a child, I talked like a child, I thought like a child, I reasoned like a child. When I became a man, I put childish ways behind me" (I Corinthians 13:11).

I am relieved to be growing up, finally.

John Wimber, founder of the Vineyard Church movement, often prayed, "Lord, help me grow up before I grow old."

Good prayer.

THINK ABOUT IT

1. Is there a character issue that God is asking you to "grow" through? Write it out.

2. Do you recognize coping mechanisms in your life? List them. Face them.

3. Do you identify with being free? What defects are you free from? Write out your story like I have so that it remains with you and you may use it to help others.

CHAPTER ELEVEN

A New Name

Throughout the Old and New Testament of the Bible, the name a person was given at birth often described the character of that person or the character the parents attributed to that child. The name could also depict a call of God on the person's life. A name often represented who the person would become. Your birth name said a lot about you and the life you had yet to live.

The Bible also reveals the stories of several important people who received a name change because God was making changes in their lives. God was intervening with His plan for their life.

One of those people who received a name change was Abraham. Originally, his name was Abram, which meant "exalted father." Then when God's time was right God came and called him, Abraham, "father of a multitude" (Genesis 17:5). His new name revealed a new future.

The reason for the name change was that a covenant was being made. God was making a covenant with Abram that said God would be God to Abraham and his descendants forever. God was making an everlasting covenant with Abraham and this act of God changed Abram and the purpose of his life. The new name was the mark of a new life. Abraham became the father of the people of God upon the earth.

Sarai was Abram's wife and she, too, received a new name. Sarai would bear the promised child, the child of covenant from God. Her new name was Sarah. She went from being "head woman" to being "princess or queen." As she bore the covenant child of God, her name seemed to change only slightly, but her reputation changed enormously, for previously she was a barren woman and in her culture this condition brought her much shame. But God had made a covenant and gave her a whole new position and purpose. God removed her shame and gave her new life (Genesis 17:15).

Sarah and Abraham received new names for new purpose. The purposes of God would be fulfilled through their lives as they obeyed Him.

Another Old Testament person who dramatically received a name change was Jacob, the son of Isaac, the grandson of Abraham. The name, Jacob, means "supplanter or deceiver." Jacob was a man who tricked his father and brother, stealing his brother's birthright and continuing to trick and manipulate and try to get his way throughout much of his life. But then in Genesis 32 we find that Jacob became tired of himself and sought God for change. He and God wrestled and Jacob yielded his human nature to God and with it came a new name.

Jacob cried out to God to bless him and God's blessing for him was a new name. God said that Jacob, "the deceiver", would now be known as Israel, "Prince of God, He Strives with God, May God Persevere." Quite a name change! Quite a new character!

Jacob emerged from his encounter with God with not only a new name and a new character but with a different body as well. From that day forward, he walked with a limp. The limp revealed that the hand of God was on his life. The limp represented his new nature of humility and dependence upon God.

When you yield yourself to God and let Him give you a new nature, you will walk differently as well. You will not go where you used to go nor do what you used to do. People will notice a new way of walking in your life. You will no longer walk the way of this world.

Your new character will cause you to walk away from the old people and places. You will walk out of independence and into family. You will walk away from an argument and into peace. You will walk from laziness into responsibility. You will walk from pride and self-reliance into obedience and submission to God.

Your walk will change in so many ways as you are led by your new name and new character. God promises us through our relationship with Christ that we will become new. 2 Corinthians 5:17 says it this way, "Therefore, if anyone is in Christ, he is a new creation; the old has gone, the new has come!"

Christ called his disciples to follow Him and learn of Him. One disciple was named Simon, Simon Bar-Jonah. This name meant "the name of nine." We could say that Simon was just an ordinary guy, no one special, just one of the gang. But we see that as Simon walked with Christ changes were taking place within him and he began to think differently. Maybe just like what is happening with you.

When Simon revealed a new way of thinking as a result of walking with Christ, Christ gave him a new name. Matthew 16:18-19 says, "And I tell you that you are Peter, and on this rock I will build my church, and the gates of Hades will not overcome it. And I will give you the keys of the kingdom of heaven, and whatever you bind on earth will be bound in heaven; and whatever you loose on earth will be loosed in heaven."

Peter was a new name of strength, stability, and significance.

Peter then had another remarkable encounter with Christ that so reveals God's heart and gives hope. As Christ prepares his disciples for His crucifixion, He has this interaction with Peter in Luke 22:31-32, "'Simon, Simon, Satan has asked to sift you as wheat. But I have prayed for you, Simon, that your faith may not fail. And when you have turned back, strengthen your brothers.' But he replied, 'Lord, I am ready to go with you to prison and to death.' Jesus answered, 'I tell you, Peter, before the rooster crows today, you will deny three times that you know me.'"

Look closely at the names that Christ uses as he addresses Peter. In this encounter, Christ used both of Peter's names. First he says, "Simon, Simon," revealing that Peter is going to revert to his old character when life gets difficult.

Can you identify with that? You think you are changing and are beginning to feel good about yourself, then a major life situation comes along and you go right back to your old ways of coping with life. We all have been just like Simon.

As Christ is revealing to Peter that he is going to be weak, Peter can't believe it. Peter tries to reassure Christ. It is like he is saying, "No way, Jesus, remember I am the Rock now. You can count on me. I am stable and strong." But Christ knows there is a spiritual battle over Peter's life and that the enemy of Peter's life wants to defeat him.

Christ reveals that He sees what Peter cannot see and that He has prayed for Peter. It is at this point that Jesus uses the name, "Peter" again.

In my words, Christ is saying to Peter, "Oh, my friend, your old nature is not totally gone and you will be weak again, but I am committed to you and I am praying and you will come through this stronger than ever. Trust in me, Peter."

Christ calls him Peter even though he is going to behave like Simon.

I take such hope in this. I know that I, too, am a disciple of Christ and that Christ keeps His focus on who I am becoming in spite of the times I revert back to my old character. Christ is faithful to us even when we are unfaithful to Him. Hallelujah!

Hebrews 7: 25 reassures us that Christ is also continually interceding for you and for me. So, just as He prayed for Peter and said that Peter would be strong again, Christ is committed to whom He says that we are becoming and continues to call us into it. Even though we may revert back to our old character and live out of our old nature at times, Christ is faithfully praying for us and calling us by our new name.

Revelation 2:17 says, "He who has an ear, let him hear what the Spirit says to the churches. To him who overcomes I will give some of the hidden manna to eat. And I will give him a white stone, and on the stone a new name is written which no one knows except him who receives it.'" (NKJV)

The Apostle Paul, who is considered the greatest apostle who ever lived, reveals the same struggle that Peter had. In Romans 7:15 and 18, Paul reveals the struggle, "I do not understand what I do. For what I want to do I do not do, but what I hate I do. For I have the desire to do what is good, but I cannot carry it out."

I am so thankful for Paul's honesty. This great man of God struggled with the same human nature we each struggle with. In verse 24 he exclaims, "What a wretched man I am! Who will rescue me from this body of death?"

Paul then continues in Romans 7 and 8 to reveal that through our relationship with Christ we are not condemned but that the

Spirit of Christ is at work within us changing us and that we are more than conquerors through Christ and that nothing can separate us from the love of God.

As a religious man, Paul (Saul) thought he could earn God's acceptance. As the apostle, he understood his dependence on Christ. Paul was no longer striving through the law but surrendered to the love of God in Christ Jesus.

Paul was a new man, relating to God in a whole new way through Christ.

Diane Fink, a ministry director at Aglow International and a friend of mine, has also changed her name. I remember several years ago when she began to ask people to no longer call her Dee, which I thought was a cool name, but to call her Diane. She explained to us that God was speaking to her about her identity. Dee was the nickname she had from her very difficult and dysfunctional childhood. The Lord was calling her by her true name, Diane which means "Divine One."

As Diane grew in God and was used by God, He wanted her to recognize and identify with the new redeemed person she was becoming. She was no longer the kid from New York who was rough and wounded. She was His "Divine One." Diane's new name truly reflects her new nature in Christ.

Christ has a new name, new life, and a new relationship for you.

In Isaiah 62, God reveals that you are:

My Delight
Married
Sought After
Not Forsaken
The Holy People
Redeemed of the Lord

THINK ABOUT IT

1. What has been your old/former name?

2. What new name do you identify with?

3. How have you seen Christ faithfully calling you into your new nature?

4. Do you ever feel, like Peter, that there is a battle between your two names?

5. Like Jacob - Israel, how has your walk changed?

CHAPTER TWELVE

Proven

I started this journey to examine character in a group that was working through Principle Five and Step Six of a Christian Recovery program.

Principle Five says: *Voluntarily submit to every change God wants to make in my life and humbly ask Him to remove my character defects.*

Step Six says: *We were entirely ready to have God remove all these defects of character.*

These two challenges – submission and change – are the very core of good discipleship, which is to make us like Jesus.

You may be aware that God's Word says His ways are not our ways (Isaiah 55:8). His way of removing our defects, making us His disciples, is probably not the way you would choose. We mentioned the Apostle Paul at the end of the last chapter. God took Paul from being a powerful religious man to knocking him off his horse, removing his sight, and then having him live away from most other people for a few years. God's process was probably not what Paul would have chosen.

I like to remember what I call the big "NEVERTHELESS" that Jesus declared when submitting to God's ways in the Garden of Gethsemane. Jesus said,

"Nevertheless, not what I will, but what You will"

(Mark 14:36 NKJV).

Romans 5:3-5 shows us part of the plan:

"but we also exult in our tribulations, knowing that tribulations brings about perseverance; and perseverance, proven character; and proven character, hope; and hope does not disappoint, because the love of God has been poured out within our hearts through the Holy Spirit who was given to us." (NASB)

This means that we will experience difficulties that help us grow. We rejoice in suffering not because we enjoy pain or deny its difficulty, but because we know God is using all of this to develop His character in us. This is what happened in my personal story about growing.

Proven character is God's goal in us.

What does "proven" mean? Dokime is the Greek word for proven and it means the process of proving or refining.

Psalm 66:10 says, "For You, O God, have tested us; You have refined us as is silver is refined" (NKJV).

Throughout the Old Testament there are references to God being a refiner who refines His people. The prophets and writers of the Word of God were familiar with refiners producing fine gold and silver and probably marveled at the process and the finished product. Then God revealed to them that His work in them was the same.

The process works this way. The refiner builds a fire and places the silver or gold in a vessel over the fire. He increases the heat and watches. As the gold or silver is heated, it melts, and the impurities float to the top and are skimmed off. This process is repeated over and over and each time the refiner peers into the liquid metal. This is the key part of the process. The refiner is looking for his own image in the metal. When the refiner sees his own reflection and no impurities, then he knows the gold or silver is refined.

Our master refiner, God Almighty, works the same way. He allows the issues of life to heat up. He watches in love, ready to remove the defects of character that rise to the surface. He watches and skims, peering each time to see if our life reflects His image.

Christ in you is the hope of glory! (Colossians 1:27)

This is the skilled process of our master refiner. He uses the fires of our life to change us, refine us, perfect us. 1Peter 1:6-7 says it so well, "In this you greatly rejoice, though now for a little while you may have had to suffer grief in all kinds of trials. These have come so that your faith–of greater worth than gold, which perishes even though refined by fire–may be proved genuine and may result in praise, glory and honor when Jesus Christ is revealed."

God says we are of greater worth than even gold.

You are worth refining.

Character defects cheapen your life.

Refining enhances your worth, increases your value.

I love the message of James 1: 2-4 from the Amplified Bible: "Consider it wholly joyful, my brethren, whenever you are enveloped in or encounter trials of any sort or fall into various temptations. Be assured and understand that the trial and proving of your faith bring out endurance and steadfastness and patience. But let endurance and steadfastness and patience have full play and do a thorough work, so that you may be perfectly and fully developed [with no defects], lacking in nothing."

Embrace the refining process. It is the perfect process for you. Only refining removes defects and reveals proven character –
His image revealed in you.

Proven character will develop no other way.

And you are worth the best!

THINK ABOUT IT

1. What difficult time has God used to prove you? List the time or times.

2. What was the proving process like for you? Write it out.

3. Name one way you are more like Christ because of the fires God has used in your life.

CHAPTER THIRTEEN

The Heart

"Man looks on the outward appearance, but the Lord looks at the heart"
(1Samuel 16:7).

God spoke these words when He commissioned Samuel to anoint
young David as King of Israel. To the human eye David did not seem
to be the one; but God was looking for a heart that was "after His
own heart" (1Samuel 13:14).

That is why refining is necessary. It reveals our heart and God looks
for His image in our heart.

Proverbs 4:23 offers a challenge to us, "Above all else, guard your
heart, for it is the wellspring of life"(NIV). "Above all else, guard your
heart, for it affects everything you do" (NLT).

In her book, *You Are Captivating/Celebrating A Mother's Heart,* Stasi
Eldredge says, "God knows that our heart is core to who we are. It is the
source of all creativity, courage, and conviction. It is the fountainhead of
our faith, our hope, and of course, our love. This wellspring of life within
us is the very essence of our existence, the center of our being."

As I think about the heart, I realize that most of us recognize the im-
portance of the health of our physical hearts. We get regular heart check-
ups, we check our blood pressure, we do cardiac exercise, and we monitor
our cholesterol to keep blood flowing to the heart.

We are encouraged to guard the well-being of our physical heart. But how often do we think to guard the heart of our soul, our innermost being?

The next few lines are excerpts from the book, *Waking the Dead*, by John Eldredge (Stasi's husband). John has a strong understanding of how central our heart is to all that is happening in our life:

"We are born on a battlefield. We were born into a world at war; a war against your heart." (page 18)

"The story of your life is the story of the long and brutal assault on your heart by the one who knows what you could be and fears it. " (page 34)

"You will not think clearly about your life until you see with the eyes of your heart." (page 34)

The subject of the heart is addressed in the Bible more than any other topic – more than works of service, more than belief or obedience, more than money, and even more than worship. Consider these verses:

"Love the Lord your God with all your heart and with all your soul and with all your strength" (Deuteronomy 6:5).

"Trust in the Lord with all your heart and lean not on your own understanding" (Proverbs 3: 5).

"Your word I have treasured in my heart, that I may not sin against You" (Psalm 119: 11 NASB).

"These people honor me with their lips, but their hearts are far from me" (Matthew 15: 8).

"All a man's ways seem right to him, but the Lord weighs the heart" (Proverbs 21: 2).

"Blessed are the pure in heart, for they will see God"
(Matthew 5:8).

"For where your treasure is, there your heart will be also"
(Luke 12:24).

And I love this one – **"For the eyes of the Lord range throughout the earth to strengthen those whose hearts are fully committed to him"** (2 Chronicles 16: 9).

According to Scripture, your heart can be troubled, wounded, pierced, grieved, even broken. It can be wise or foolish, cheerful, joyful, merry and glad. It can be steadfast, true, upright, stout, valiant or frightened, faint or cowardly. It can be wondering, forgetful, dull, stubborn, proud, hardened, wicked, and perverse. But worst of all, it can be divided.

Your heart is the very essence of your existence, the center of your being, the fount of your life.

The thoughts and intents of the heart shape your life. Proverbs 23:7 (NKJV) says it simply, **"For as he thinks in his heart, so he is."**

Your heart is the center of your emotions and of your deepest thinking. Hebrews 4:12 says this about the Word of God: **"Sharper than any double-edged sword, it penetrates even to dividing soul and spirit, joints and marrow; it judges the thoughts and attitudes of the heart."**

The thoughts and intents of the heart are what shape a person's life. Your character is determined by your motives and your motives are a matter of your heart.

In his teaching series, *The Utter Relief of Holiness,* John Eldredge examines the motives of his heart and ours. He says first of all that

Jesus told the Pharisees that if they would clean the inside of the cup the whole cup would be clean (Matthew 23:25-26). Jesus moves from the inside to outside, from the heart to behavior.

Eldredge asks a series of heart-examining questions:

Why do we pray? – to be heard by others or to truly relate to God?

Why do we fast? why do we give? – to be seen by man or by God?

Why don't we answer the phone? – are we truly busy or avoiding?

Why go to church? – to really worship or to be seen by others?

Why do we want our children to behave in public? – for their good or because of what people will think of us as parents?

Why do we dress the way we do? – to be noticed or to be comfortable? Etc.

He goes on to honestly admit that he chose to fast from public speaking for 6 months because he realized that even though he was speaking on Biblical things, his motive was for personal approval and acceptance. He then shares that because of childhood wounds he is a driven man and that he would come home at the end of the day and have a drink. It became a pattern in his life. It was his way of unwinding from the pressures of the day. He did not even think to ask God to comfort him; he used alcohol as his comforter. Now that he has seen his drinking pattern, he is going to God for comfort and peace and has not had a drink in months. Examining his motives changed him from the inside out.

As John Eldredge honestly examined the motives of his heart, it became freeing for him. He says that "it opens fields of goodness." It feels good to be free of wrong motives and to have a clean heart.

King David was not a perfect person; he sinned many times. But his heart was after God's. He wanted to have a right heart even though he did not always do the right things. This gives us hope. God loved David and continued to convict David's heart of his sins and give him opportunities to choose a new heart. This was the key. David would repent; he cried out to God, "Create in me a pure heart, O God, and renew a steadfast spirit within me" (Psalm 51:10).

I love the way this reads in *The Message*:

"What you're after is truth from the inside out. Enter me, then; conceive a new, true life."

You cannot be the person God created you to be and you cannot live the life He purposed for you, unless your heart is after His heart. Like David, cry out to God. He will answer.

Christ came to ransom your heart so it could be like His.

THINK ABOUT IT

1. What area of your heart do you know is "after God's"? How do you know?

2. What area of your heart do you know God is working to make like His?

3. How do you identify with the battle for your heart?

4. Are you surprised by what you see when you examine the motives of your heart?

CHAPTER FOURTEEN

Transformed

Insanity is defined as doing the same thing over and over, expecting a different result. We live this insane way when sin and defects are ruling our lives. We repeat the same behaviors, reap the same consequences of chaos in our lives, and continue the downward spiral of confusion.

To decide to voluntarily let God remove my defects means no more insane thinking. I am no longer justifying wrong behavior and thinking. I recognize that my coping mechanisms have been self-defeating. I am confessing that I need change.

When I let God remove my defects I am being transformed. I am no longer thinking that my stubbornness or anger, self-pity and perfectionism work for me. I have had a change of mind.

My mind is now agreeing with God that these old ways, even though familiar and comfortable, are not beneficial. I now recognize that they are my problem and that my life will continue to be filled with difficulty as long as I keep thinking and doing the same old things.

Jimmy Evans, a pastor and leader of Marriage Today, a highly effective ministry to marriages, writes, "The truth is, we all come to critical times in our lives when we must make decisions as to which way we will turn. Will we forgive or hold a grudge? Will we stay and work things out or run from our problems? In life, there are many proverbial 'forks in the road'. In my opinion, what we do at these times forms our character and forges our destinies." ("Weekly Marriage Builder," November 18, 2007, Jimmy Evans-Marriage Today, jimmy@marriagetoday.org)

God has His wisdom for us in Romans 12:2a, "Do not conform any longer to the pattern of this world, but be transformed by the renewing of your mind."

The Message is so good with this – "Don't become so well-adjusted to your culture that you fit into it without even thinking. Instead, fix your attention on God. You'll be changed from the inside out. Readily recognize what he wants from you, and quickly respond to it. Unlike the culture around you, always dragging you down to its level of immaturity, God brings the best out of you, develops well-formed maturity in you."

A renewed mind with a refined heart creates a new life. It is God's will for each of us.

Adam and Eve listened to the voice of the deceiver, but we have the voice of the Redeemer speaking consistently to us through His Word. It is our choice to listen to the power of His truth and have the cycle of insanity broken.

With a new heart we are able to hear the truth that transforms our minds and make the choices that reveal the transformation of our character!

THINK ABOUT IT

1. When were you at a "fork in the road" in your thinking?

2. What did your decision reveal about your character?

3. What insane pattern needs to be submitted to God at this time in your life?

4. What part of your thinking is most transformed through this teaching?

CHAPTER FIFTEEN

The Will

We have mentioned hinges before. Here is another one, perhaps the most significant.

The soul is generally considered a composite of the mind, will, and emotions. Of these three dynamics, we seem to be conscious of our emotions and also of our mind because we are familiar with feelings and thoughts. But the will is the more obscure part of the soul.

Emotions we feel and even see at times. Thoughts we are usually conscious of. In a sense, we are "in touch" with our thoughts and feelings, but our will, most of the time, seems out of reach. We know we have it but we don't give it much consideration. Yet it is the hinge of the soul.

The will determines the direction of our choices, our actions, our life. Our emotions let us know how we feel about things such as a problem or an opportunity. Our thoughts tell us what we think, positive or negative. But the will is the hinge that chooses yes or no.

We talk about changing our mind and changing our feelings, but to change either one we really have to change our will. We have to move in another direction.

I think you get the idea.

I love Webster's definition of the will. The will is conscious power, the power of choice, volition, determination, resolution and more. Power is in the will, power for good or evil, right or wrong, life or death. The will is mighty, and so much hinges on which direction we take it.

What disturbs me about this whole issue of the will is how little we seem to recognize it operating within us. In some situations we are conscious of exercising our willpower, such as dieting, exercising, and disciplining ourselves in various ways. This is good. But how often do we discipline ourselves in our moral or spiritual choices? How consistently and consciously do we set our will to obey God or the law or even just good manners?

We should consciously choose who we will be in situations moment by moment, day by day. Someone struggling with addiction must set their will consistently to avoid what triggers their addiction. They must avoid certain people, talk, places and thoughts.

Self-discipline is the will at work, consciously and deliberately.

Our thoughts and feelings are ever in competition for the control of our will. They are like siblings vying for the driver's seat (my twin sister and I did that.) Each feels equally significant and is sure they are the most important at the moment. Who will win? Who is stronger? Some people are always doing what they "feel" while others are ever analyzing, unable to decide.

We must be conscious of our will. We must deliberately and decisively make conscious choices based not just on feelings, which change so easily, nor on thoughts which may not be accurate. Our will must be controlled by something more sure, more concrete, more stable. Our will must be hinged to something upright and secure. The Word of God is a good anchor. It is unchanging and infallible.

Jesus was both fully man and fully God. The man-Christ struggled with His will. In the Garden of Gethsemane, He had to decide to either be controlled by His feelings, circumstances, and fears or by the will of God. We know He finally surrendered with these words, "'not as I will but as you will'" (Matthew 26: 39). Even Jesus had to consciously choose the direction of His will.

His choice was eternally great for us but immediately difficult for Him. He suffered and died.

Thankfully, He set His will according to something higher and more significant than circumstances or feelings–the very will of God Almighty. This should consistently be our standard as well–letting God be Lord of our lives. It sounds so right and good, yet is so difficult.

Ask the codependent, the one who is the people-pleaser, the one who is afraid of upsetting others.

It can be so difficult to risk the anger or disapproval of significant people even when we know that what they want from us is not right.

Please God or man? Should be a no-brainer but certainly is not. The codependent will serve the person they need or fear. I know. I have been there. I have been that codependent justifying serving man, not God. God let me know it was idolatry. Idolatry is worshipping and serving the created rather than the Creator (Romans 1:25). Or if I am the controlling codependent and I am manipulating people and situations out of my fear, then I am trying to be God rather than trusting God with His job and my life. This is the idolatry of self that can be expressed in many ways.

The love of self rules the will of many. Self must have what it wants. It might be excessive eating, drinking, gambling, shopping, sleep, anger, control, or sex. Self just must be satisfied regardless of the consequences of obesity, addiction, job loss, relationship failure, abuse, arrest, isolation, etc.

The truth is, God's will is always right for us. He sees the end from the beginning (Revelation 21:6) and His will is righteous, good and true. God is trustworthy. He never fails, falls short, or is wrong. God has a proven track record.

It is time to turn our life, which includes our will, over to the care and control of God. I love these words. This is the way Principle Three from the Eight Principles of Recovery says it:

"Consciously choose to commit all my life and will to Christ's care and control."

Step Three of the Twelve Steps and their Biblical Comparisons says:

"We made a decision to turn our lives and our wills over to the care of God."

You see through these Principles and Steps that we make a choice to turn our will over to God. So we decide with our mind and then choose with our will whether we submit our will.

Submitting to the care and control of an all-loving God is great wisdom.

I will close with a question. Has submitting your will to anyone or anything else really worked for you? Probably not. I encourage you to be wise and submit your will to the will of God. It was wisdom for Jesus and is wisdom for you.

Make this willful choice today and tomorrow and the day after, and the next and the next....

Your character and destiny hinge on the conscious positioning of your will.

THINK ABOUT IT

1. Are you more controlled by your feelings or your thinking? Are you emotional or analytical?

2. When did you last consciously choose the direction of your will? What was the situation and what was the outcome?

3. In what situation today do you consciously need to set your will? Are you aware of God's will in the situation?

4. Have you made a decision to turn your life and will over to the care and control of Christ?

CHAPTER SIXTEEN

All Things New....

The shape of my new character is the shape of my new future

I started this journey with questions and I now believe I have discovered some answers. I hope you have as well.

I now can distinguish between my behavior and my character. I now know that my character is my choice. I understand that my character can be displayed through my temperament and personality, but they do not determine my character. I recognize that my wounds may have marked me in the past, but they do not have to shape my future.

Most of all, I now know that God cares and wants to help. He knows exactly how to remove my defects of character.

I have the privilege of submitting to the changes He wants to make in me.

He is proving me and forming His very own character in me!

Understanding the process and knowing what God wants makes all the difference.

God is asking that we submit to the loving work of His heart in our hearts.

The process of change is challenging but entirely worth it all.

The Maker, says, " 'Behold, I make all things new'" (Revelation 21:5 NKJV).

THINK ABOUT IT

1. As you have learned about your character, what is now new in you?

2. What do you expect to be new in your future as a result of your new character?

Prayer

"Lord, thank you for giving me wisdom and understanding about my character. I now know that the changes You want to make in me are also what I want.

With the assurance of Your love, I voluntarily submit to every change You want to make in my life and I humbly ask You to remove my defects of character.

I look forward to my new character and all the freedom it will bring for my future."

Amen

The following Character Qualities are adapted by Rod Handley and his ministry, Character That Counts. They have given us permission to use their work. We greatly encourage you to visit their website: www.characterthatcounts.org for more of their encouraging ministry dedicated to building integrity and character in God's Kingdom.

100+ CHARACTER QUALITIES

ALERTNESS: Being keenly aware of the events taking place around me so that I can have the right responses to them.

ATTENTIVENESS: Showing the worth of a person or task by giving my undivided concentration.

AVAILABILITY: Making my own schedule and priorities secondary to the wishes of those I serve.

BENEVOLENCE: Giving to others' basic needs without expectations of personal reward.

BOLDNESS: Demonstrating the confidence and courage that doing what is right will bring ultimate victory regardless of present opposition.

BREADTH: Having depth and broadness, in words and deeds, within the heart and mind.

BROTHERLINESS: Exhibiting a kinship and disposition to render help because of a relationship.

CANDOR: Speaking the truth at the time when the truth should be spoken. This is done through openness, fairness and sincerity.

CAUTION: Knowing to be alert and prudent in a hazardous or dangerous situation.

CHEERFUL: Expressing encouragement, approval and/or congratulations at the proper time.

CHIVALRY: Protecting the weak, the suffering and the neglected by maintaining justice and rightness.

COMMITMENT: Devoting myself to following up on my words (promises, pledges or vows) with action.

COMPASSION: Investing whatever is necessary to heal the hurts of others by the willingness to bear their pain.

CONFIDENCE: Placing full trust and belief in the reliability of a person or thing.

CONSISTENCY: Following constantly the same principles, course or form in all circumstances; holding together.

CONTENTMENT: Accepting myself as God created me with my gifts, talents, abilities and opportunities.

COURAGE: Fulfilling my responsibilities and standing up for convictions in spite of being afraid.

CREATIVITY: Approaching a need, a task or an idea from a new perspective.

DECISIVENESS: Learning to finalize difficult decisions on the basis of what is right, not popular or tempting.

DEFERENCE: Limiting my freedom to speak and act in order to not offend the tastes of others.

DEPENDABILITY: Fulfilling what I consented to do even if it means unexpected sacrifice.

DETERMINATION: Working intently to accomplish goals regardless of the opposition.

DILIGENCE: Visualizing each task as a special assignment and using all my energies to accomplish it.

DISCERNMENT: Seeking to use intuitive ability to judge situations and people; understanding why things happen to me and others.

DISCIPLINE: Receiving instruction and correction in a positive way; maintaining and enforcing proper conduct in accordance with the guidelines and rules.

DISCRETION: Recognizing and avoiding words, actions and attitudes which could result in undesirable consequences.

ENDURANCE: Exercising inward strength to withstand stress and do my best in managing what occurs in my life.

ENTHUSIASM: Expressing lively, absorbing interest in each task as I give it my best effort.

FAIRNESS (EQUITY): Looking at a decision from the viewpoint of each person involved.

FAITH: Developing an unshakable confidence in God and acting upon it.

FAITHFULNESS: Being thorough in the performance of my duties; being true to my words, promises and vows.

FEAR OF THE LORD: Having a sense of awe and respect for Almighty God which goes above and beyond anyone else or anything.

FIRMNESS: Exerting a tenacity of will with strength and resoluteness. A willingness to run counter to the traditions and fashions of the world.

FLEXIBILITY: Learning how to cheerfully change plans when unexpected conditions require it.

FORGIVENESS: Clearing the record of those who have wronged me and not holding their past offenses against them.

FRIENDSHIP: Coming alongside another person for mutual support and encouragement.

GENEROSITY: Realizing that all I have (time, talents and treasures) belongs to God and freely giving of these to benefit others.

GENTLENESS: Learning to respond to needs with kindness, personal care and love.

GLADNESS: Abounding in joy, jubilation and cheerfulness.

GOAL-ORIENTED: Achieving maximum results toward the area where my effort is directed.

GOODNESS: Having moral excellence and a virtuous lifestyle; a general quality of proper conduct.

GRATEFULNESS: Making known to others by my words and actions how they have benefited my life.

GREATNESS: Demonstrating an extraordinary capacity for achievement.

HOLINESS: Having no blemish or stain. Being whole with no trace of regret or remorse.

HONESTY: Proclaiming the truth with sincerity and frankness in all situations.

HONOR: Respecting those in leadership because of the higher authorities they represent.

HOPE: Feeling that my deepest desire will be realized and that events will turn out for the best.

HOSPITALITY: Sharing cheerfully food, shelter and my life with those whom I come in contact.

HUMILITY: Seeing the contrast between what is perfect and my inability to achieve that perfection.

INDIGNATION: Channeling the driving passion of righteous anger without sinning.

INITIATIVE: Recognizing and doing what needs to be done before I am asked to do it.

INTEGRITY: Being whole and complete in moral and ethical principles.

JOYFULNESS: Knowing how to be pleasant regardless of the outside circumstances which ultimately lifts the spirits of others.

JUSTICE: Taking personal responsibility to uphold what is pure, right and true.

KINDNESS: Demonstrating a gentle, sympathetic attitude towards others.

KNOWLEDGE: Becoming acquainted with facts, truths or principles through study and investigation.

LEADERSHIP: Guiding others toward a positive conclusion.

LOVE: Having a deep personal attachment and affection for another person.

LOYALTY: Using difficult times to demonstrate my commitment to others or to what is right.

MEEKNESS: Yielding my power, personal rights and expectations humbly with a desire to serve.

NARROWNESS: Staying within established boundaries and limits.

OBEDIENCE: Fulfilling instructions so that the one I am serving will be fully satisfied and pleased.

OPTIMISM: Endeavoring to see all the possibilities and capacities of the human heart; confident, hopeful and never doubtful.

ORDERLINESS: Learning to organize and care for personal possessions to achieve greater efficiency.

ORIGINALITY: Creating "new" thinking, ideas and expanding truths from an independent viewpoint.

PASSIONATE: Having an intense, powerful or compelling emotion and feelings towards others or something.

PATIENCE: Accepting difficult situations and without demanding a deadline to remove it.

PEACEFULNESS: Being at rest with myself and others.

PERSUASIVENESS: Guiding another's mental roadblocks by using words which cause the listener's spirit to confirm the spoken truth.

POISE: Being totally balanced in mind, body and spirit.

PRAYERFUL: Communing with God spiritually through adoration, confession, thanksgiving and supplication.

PROSPERITY: Flourishing or being successful, especially pertaining to financial issues.

PRUDENCE: Exhibiting caution, humbleness and wisdom in regards to practical matters.

PUNCTUALITY: Showing respect for other people by respectfully using the limited time they have.

PURE SPEECH: Speaking words that are clean, spotless and without blemish.

PURITY: Freeing yourself from anything that contaminates or adulterates.

PURPOSEFUL: Exercising determination to stay on track until the goal is achieved.

REASONABLENESS: Having a sound mind by being level headed, sane and demonstrating common sense.

RESOURCEFULNESS: Using wisely that which others would normally overlook or discard.

RESPECT: Honoring and esteeming another person due to deep admiration.

RESPONSIBILITY: Knowing and doing what is expected from me.

REVERENCE: Learning to give honor where it is due and to respect the possessions and property of others.

RIGHTEOUSNESS: Acting in a moral and upright way that honors God, regardless of who is watching.

SECURITY: Structuring my life around what is eternal and cannot be destroyed or taken away.

SELF-CONTROL: Bringing my thoughts, words, actions and attitudes into constant obedience in order to benefit others.

SENSITIVITY: Being aware and attentive to the true attitudes and emotional needs of those around me.

SERVANTHOOD: Caring for and meeting the needs of others before caring for myself.

SINCERITY: Endeavoring to do what is right, without ulterior motives.

STEWARDSHIP: Administering and managing personal and financial affairs effectively.

TEACHABILITY: Demonstrating a willingness to learn or be trained without any reservations or hindrances.

THANKFULNESS: Expressing deep gratitude and appreciation to people and to God.

THOROUGHNESS: Executing something perfectly with the realization that each of my tasks will be reviewed.

THOUGHTFULNESS: Showing consideration for others through acts of kindness and/or words.

THRIFTINESS: Preventing not letting myself or others spend that which is not necessary.

TOLERANCE: Learning to accept others as valuable individuals regardless of their maturity.

TRANSPARENCY: Allowing others to shine a light on my life for the purpose of being accountable.

TRUTHFULNESS: Earning future trust by accurately reporting past facts.

TRUST or TRUSTWORTHY: Believing completely and totally in someone or something.

UNDERSTANDING: Exhibiting strong intelligence and a sound mind in comprehending and discerning matters.

VIRTUE: Learning to build personal moral standards which will cause others to desire a greater moral life.

VISIONARY: Dreaming not inhibited by the unknown. Looking beyond problems by creating successful solutions.

VULNERABILITY: Being open to receive constructive criticism and guidance.

WISDOM: Learning to see and respond correctly to life situations with keen judgment; the application of knowledge.

WORSHIP: Honoring God reverently.

Adapted from several sources including "Institute in Basic Conflicts" by Bruce Bickel; Character First! program and "The Character of Jesus" by Charles Edward Jefferson.

WORKS CITED

Baker, John. *Celebrate Recovery Updated Participants Guide Set (CELEBRATE RECOVERY)*. Grand Rapids, Michigan: Zondervan, 2005.

Baker, John. *Life's Healing Choices: Freedom from Your Hurts, Hang-ups, and Habits*. West Monroe: Howard Books, 2007.

Clark, Beth, and Mary Forsythe. *A Glimpse of Grace: A True Story*. New York: Crossstaff Publishers, 2004.

Cottle, Ronald. *Anointed to Reign*. New Jersey: Destiny Image Publishers, 1996.

Eldredge, John. *Waking the Dead: The Glory of a Heart Fully Alive*. Waco, TX: Thomas Nelson, 2006.

Eldredge, Staci. *You Are Captivating*. Nashville, TN: Thomas Nelson, 2007.

Hansen Hoyt, Jane . *Fashioned for Intimacy*. Ventura, California: Regal Books, 1997.

Max, Tucker. *I Hope They Serve Beer In Hell*. New York: Citadel Press, 2006.

Strong, James. *Strong's Exhaustive Concordance.* Peabody Massachusetts: Hendrickson Publishers, 2007.

Wilhite, Mike Foster & Jud. *Deadly Viper Character Assassins*. California: Ethur, 2007.

Robert Burns (Everyman Poetry Library). London: Everyman Paperback Classics, 1997.

CONTACT INFORMATION

Jennie Newbrough, D.Min.

3708 Woodlawn Way, Weirton, WV 26062

Phone 304.797.1198 or 304.224.6955

Email: hwccc@msn.com

Jennie Newbrough serves Aglow International as the Educational Resource Specialist. An author, she has written the Aglow Support Group Leader's Guide that has been used to train leaders the across the nation. While serving as the Aglow Relationship Resource Person she developed the Care Group network for the Aglow ministry. As a teacher of God's Word, Jennie has taught at Aglow fellowships throughout the United States, in Bible studies, churches, seminars and retreats.

Jennie earned a Doctorate of Ministry, Masters of Theology and Masters of Divinity from Christian Life School of Theology. She also founded and directed a local campus of Christian Life School of Theology. Jennie also has a Bachelors Degree in secondary education from West Liberty State College.

For the past 25 years Jennie has been a Pastoral Counselor. She founded His Word Christian Counseling to offer Christian counseling and teaching to the body of Christ. She counsels at the Vineyard Church in Wheeling, WV and Crossroads UMC in Oakdale, PA. Jennie has studied at the Institute of Pastoral Counseling in Akron, OH and is a member of the American Association of Christian Counselors. She is ordained through International Seminary in Plymouth, FL.

In her home church, The Vineyard Church of Wheeling, WV, Jennie is a counselor and the Ministry Leader of Celebrate Recovery, a Christian 12 Step program.

As a member of the Board of Directors of Words of Life Ministries, an international prayer ministry, Jennie has traveled and ministered in other nations.

She and her husband, John, live in Weirton, WV and have two adult children and two grandchildren

— NOTES —

— NOTES —

— NOTES —

— NOTES —

— NOTES —

— NOTES —

— NOTES —

— NOTES —

— NOTES —